# *THE*
# FEEDER

Jennifer Jackson Berry

YESYES BOOKS / PORTLAND

THE FEEDER © 2016 BY JENNIFER JACKSON BERRY

COVER ART: *DIDYMOUS (THE TWINS)* © BRENDA STUMPF
COVER & INTERIOR DESIGN: ALBAN FISCHER
LEAD EDITOR: STEVIE EDWARDS

FIRST EDITION, 2016
ISBN 978-1-936919-47-5

PRINTED IN THE UNITED STATES OF AMERICA

PUBLISHED BY YESYES BOOKS
1614 NE ALBERTA ST
PORTLAND, OR 97211
YESYESBOOKS.COM

KMA SULLIVAN, PUBLISHER
JILL KOLONGOWSKI, MANAGING EDITOR
STEVIE EDWARDS, SENIOR EDITOR, BOOK DEVELOPMENT
ALBAN FISCHER, GRAPHIC DESIGNER
BEYZA OZER, DEPUTY DIRECTOR OF SOCIAL MEDIA
AMBER RAMBHAROSE, CREATIVE DIRECTOR OF SOCIAL MEDIA
PHILLIP B. WILLIAMS, COEDITOR IN CHIEF, *VINYL*
MARK DERKS, FICTION EDITOR, *VINYL*
JOANN BALINGIT, ASSISTANT EDITOR
MARY CATHERINE CURLEY, ASSISTANT EDITOR
COLE HILDEBRAND, ASSISTANT EDITOR
JOHNNA C. GURGEL, ASSISTANT EDITOR, PUBLICITY
CARLY SCHWEPPE, ASSISTANT EDITOR, *VINYL*
HARI ZIYAD, ASSISTANT EDITOR, *VINYL*

# Contents

I Lost Our Baby · 11

This Trouble of Curls · 15

I Did Things for the Stories · 17

all day    i dream    about sex · 19

Lost & Found Love Poem with Oranges & Trash · 20

Fair: The Guesser · 21

Fat Girl Reads Her Horoscope · 22

Obedience Class · 23

Fat Girl on Baseball · 25

The Rub · 27

A Story of Girls · 28

On the Day My Husband is Assumed to be a Father by the Clerk
    in the Big & Tall Man's Clothing Store · 30

Collecting Slights · 32

The Poem About Infertility · 34

Playground · 35

The Feeder Said to Me · 39

Fat Girl at Weight Watchers Meeting · 41

Fat Girl Confuses Food & Sex, Again · 43

x = feathers, y = boards · 44

Writing the Fat Girl · 45

I just did what I always do: eat · 46

Fat Girl on Winter Beach · 48

Not Quite Taste · 49

Post-Miscarriage: Day 55 · 51

Fair: Fun House Mirror · 53

Post-Miscarriage: Day 186 · 54

Fat Girl Has Regular Sex · 56

Between My Legs & My Future · 61

Is No · 62


What I Said to the Feeder · 65

What Hunger Was · 67

Fair: Ring Toss · 68

No One Has Touched Me So Hard It Calmed Me · 69

Post-Miscarriage: Day 74 · 70

Another Poem About Infertility · 71

Even the Times I Cry · 73

My Offal Honeymoon · 74

The Infertile Couple · 75

What Not to Do · 76

Paper Birthday · 78

Contemplating a Gift for a Pregnancy Announcement · 79

Coming to Terms with Gambling & Losing · 80

Notes for Whoever Will Take Care of Us When We're Old · 81

I'm Showing · 82

I'm Telling · 84

Before & After · 86


*Acknowledgments* · 87

for Mike

I lost our baby in between the couch cushions,
under the car seat, in the trunk.
I lost our baby at Cedar Point—she was rolled up
in a plastic money holder I wore around my neck.
It looked like soap-on-a-rope & I left it
on the back of the toilet after changing wet clothes.
I lost our baby during a party—
she was on top of the fridge, then she was gone.
I lost our baby in the bottom of my purse
& when she rolled under the bed.
I lost our baby when I moved from the third floor
walk-up apartment. I lost our baby at a Good Will
drop-off site in Bloomington, Indiana.
I lost our baby when I was walking through the parking lot—
my keychain broke & she slipped right off.
I lost our baby in a friend's house fire.
I lost our baby in the dorms
when the girl across the hall borrowed her & never returned her.
I lost our baby even though I wrote my name on her,
with a cute little stamp of a teddy bear reading.
*This baby belongs to Jennifer.* I lost our baby

on trash day, on my birthday, on a Thursday.
I lost our baby in dozens of pearls bouncing
across linoleum tiles—I had her in my mouth
& the thread snapped.

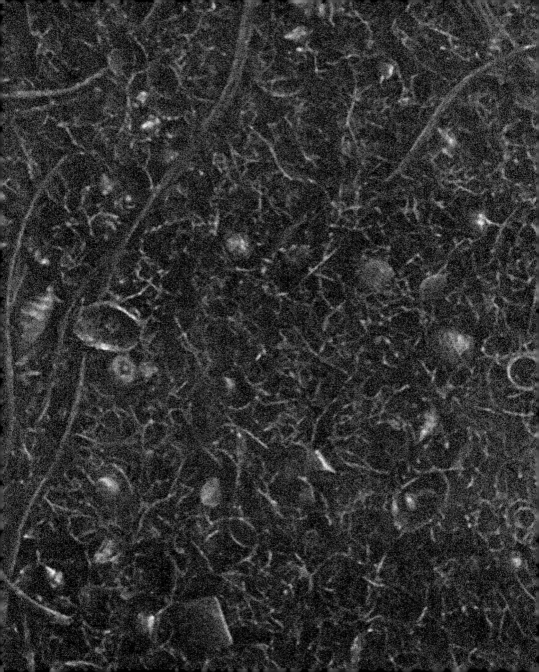

# This Trouble of Curls

A woman my age with this trouble
of curls should have a regular stylist.
I go to Supercuts. I've been broken up with
by more hairdressers than boyfriends.
Janine got fired two years ago
& didn't take my number from the rolodex.
Before her, Kate moved to Arizona
& didn't tell me. I left Tammy decades ago,
but she was begging for it.
How could she dye blonde a chunk of hair
left an inch longer than my bob,
a side-tail just above my left collar bone
& think it looked good?
My husband remembers that flax curl
from 8th grade, teases me.
He's still upset only one person noticed
when he cut his tail the next year.
He was nervous the weekend before
going back to school a different man,
his mid-back lock just a scut at his nape.
My neck is cold.

*A little off the length* didn't translate this time.
It's October so my elbows are covered.
We live in a time of three-quarter sleeves.
I grew up when it was only short sleeve
or long sleeve & the girls at Fantastic Sam's
had pet names in lights above their stations:
*Sweet Pea, Angel, Toots.*
Cookie took the thinning shears to my hair once.
She said, *Don't tell your dad I made you look 21.*
I looked like her: tough, teased.
It was the most amazing mullet
back when mullets were allowed.
I'll keep going to the chains with the just-
graduated girls. I'll hope for someone who studied.
Last week when my latest girl asked her coworker
for a Mason Pearson brush, then muttered,
*Didn't you pay attention in school?*
I knew I'd give up my head to her.

My advice: eat things mayo-based, hot
from the sun. When you puke,

puke in the port-a-potty,
bare knees & hair loose.

At the pavilion after,
take another spoonful.

But don't swat the wasp.
Let it happen. Let the sting happen.

I knelt in front of the bartender,
long after last call, sweat

on his skin saltier than any peanut
& I was always thirsty.

On Halloween, Andrew Dice Clay,
yeah, I fucked him.

But, *this* is sex sober.
*This* coupling, *this* marriage—

no makeshift togas made
before crawling out of bed,

*this* is naked.
I knew all about lying

down & covering up—
I had to learn morning

breath & body-racking sobs
while someone watched—

the things I did alone,
now displayed.

We eat what's gone
bad together,

the dead, the dying,
the never-born.

# all day     i dream     about sex

all day          i dream          about sex

          i dream          about all day sex all day
i day dream
               about sex all

day i dream          sex          about all

all about          day i dream sex
     all day i dream          about sex all day

     i     dream     about     sex     all     day
all day
          i dream all about sex all

about sex          all day          i dream

dream day     i     all about sex

# Lost & Found Love Poem with Oranges & Trash

Seven clementines line the counter.

I put the only three still firm

in my lunch bag. The segments

of the four remaining had pulled back

from the browning rind like

the brain is set back from the skull,

where blood collects post-trauma.

I cup the softened orbs.

The carpels move under that delicate, rugged covering.

& later when I look up

all kinds of oranges,

I find rind originates by a thickening

of a single ovary wall.

The fruit of any citrus tree: hesperidium, modified berries,

with seeds & flesh soft, self-fertile.

& at noon I press my thumbnail near the stem, 3x piercing

then stripping to the pith.

I will find that heady scent still

with me hours later when I touch my face.

& when I get home

the sweet fruit are buried in the trash.

# Fair: The Guesser

Leg skin stretched to shine, the boy
waddled to the scale, his father's hand
on his four-year-old back. Compassion
lived in the carnie when she guessed: *79?*
& then *Aww, you win! Go pick a prize!*
She never even whispered afterward
what 79 lowballed.

I recognized the father as my boyfriend
at 19, the man six years older who
grabbed my breasts, paws swinging
from a 400 lb. frame, *these are too big*
He did that kind of damage you can't
really describe. If I were a different person,
I might brag about being tied to the bed
for my first time.
                    I watched that man's face,
proud his son fooled his first woman
into feeling sorry for him.
My husband standing beside me in the crowd
around the game read every story in my face,
even ones I never told.

# Fat Girl Reads Her Horoscope

Virgos, perfectionists. I'll learn to control the gag reflex with something else in my mouth—an Altoid, a Hall's, a blast of Binaca. *You'll start focusing on material acquisitions more than ever before.* Virgos are good analysts & planners. I wish that reciting the alphabet while twisting an apple stem really could predict my future husband. *Love will come to the forefront, hitting a climax between Sunday night and Wednesday afternoon.* I remember in 2nd grade for eleven times in a row the stem came off on the letter H: Timmy Hunt. The last time I saw him the summer between junior & senior years of college he was waiting tables at Red Lobster. *Sex can be totally unpredictable, especially on the 21st.* I fear I'll die slowly, at the speed of an old man easing himself into the bathtub. At Red Lobster that night we waited for 45 minutes for a table—what will rival my time spent waiting for sex? *Be careful this month—what you say always seems to be the wrong thing, so you may revert to saying nothing.* I used to hear stories of stellar fucks in the back of Tim's Camaro, the chocolate interior melting under naked thighs. Virgos aren't wasteful & we don't do it for the compliments.

# Obedience Class

First session we brought the puppy,
weren't supposed to.

We're hungover, so damn
hung over. You take her back

to the car to sleep & I sit
through questions about firm hands

& being the alpha dog,
an angry mother of four asks

about crates & pads & piss.
The puppy bounds in the door first,

unbridled licking—
beer spittle off the faces

of friends sprawled on the floor.
I forgot the puppy was supposed to wait

for us, understand we are the leaders
through the threshold.

We go back to bed.
We're alpha, we throw the parties

& even when we're on all fours,
we're in control.

We don't find the threshold
all that important—

neither of us ever imagining
anything bridal.

# Fat Girl on Baseball

The fear is I'll be the catcher
who somehow opens her legs too far,
revealing the secrets of the pitch.
I remember Amy in junior high
flustered over how to avoid a hand
down her pants at a Friday night movie.
A tucked-in shirt *and* a belt was
my solution. Monday morning,
she told me she untucked
& though she didn't know what base it was,
he treated her like a baby would
his mother—his mouth on her breast.
She was able to avoid the hand.

      I never dated someone
in that high school sort of way,
never had to worry about how far to let him go
or the backseats of cars
or basements of vacationing parents
or how my life would sound scribbled

on walls above urinals or between
towel snaps in the locker room.

There's a woman at work whose
husband calls every afternoon at 3:15. She kicks
off her shoes, turns from her computer screen,
giggles: *Guess who's gonna get lucky tonight.*
Other secretaries crowd her desk,
watching her bask in the heat of love.
Sometimes I pick up instead—tell him
she isn't here, pass along some invented
message, take my turn at a 7th hour stretch.
I used to peek at Amy's notes too, before
she'd fold them into elaborate diamonds,
imagining I wrote the lines, not her.

Some methods of foreplay are safe:
paper, the phone. Years past contemplating
what base to stop at, I worry about crossing
the line of too much information.
After riding the bench for so long, the language
of the lure is what I prefer.

The man last night was a rubber, his palm like sandpaper across my back after our date. There can be intimacy in whittling, but not that. I think I might be pretty. I wonder what I'll do to deserve honey & word jumbles Sunday morning next to a cup of tea—double straw in a coke bottle image of love I want to find, but haven't. My father was conceived in a circus tent. My grandparents heeled bottle caps into the ground & thrust against each other on the makeshift tent floor, cold under feet & asses the whole month long hunting trip. There's always talk of the one that got away. I hunt straddling planes. I thought I found love at a junior high dance. Suppose there was time travel. Suppose I waltzed from sweaty gym to wedding chapel. Suppose I could get to him. I can't & no one is coming for me tonight. There's not much difference between a circus & a church, just the lengths of the beards. I smear honey on every offering & always use a scope. That's from a hunting manual & he is suspended in that memory, dancing.

# A Story of Girls

We stopped short of kissing, never

even practicing on fists in front of each other.

At sleepovers, we'd take turns:

Sarah, the flat one, never liked showing

& I had adopted the quick flash,

whipping up my shirt after a 1-2-3-look-at-me.

I had no idea the Kama Sutra describes seventeen

types of kisses. I thought the only constant for good

sex was bare flesh, that so much depended on nudity.

One afternoon behind Nicole's house

we pulled our shorts down around our ankles.

We planned to pull them back up

at the edge of the woods when her house was in sight.

We heard dirt bikes, the other fifth graders, the boys

out doing what we thought they did

on summer afternoons, racing, chasing squirrels.

I've never dressed so quickly.


I would soon realize the boys knew

even more than we did. I knew Amy

wore her day-of-the-week panties on the wrong days.

I knew one of the boys showed Nicole his thing
after she was caught in a rousing game of Boys Chase Girls.
I had jelly bracelets winding up only one wrist
because I knew any adornment on my left meant
I was available—bit of wisdom from my mother.
My hair was long & curly, sometimes still in braids,
even though I knew they weren't cool.
I hoped the boys would keep grabbing my hair
like handlebars.

Our circle disintegrated,
but I heard, because girls always heard,
some of them were going down
on first dates. It had become tighter jeans, darker panties.
Tube tops, the first clue there were such things as sex clothes.
I only wore mine at home, bedroom door closed.
I still tongued my fingers apart, still practiced
the pucker, then open. It had become real
for them. It had become gold bracelets & hair straight
as the arrows they drew through doodled hearts.

# On the Day My Husband is Assumed to be a Father by the Clerk in the Big & Tall Man's Clothing Store

I had a coupon for a free polo shirt.
The clerk suggested the bright green & I said
I don't think he'll go for that. I chose navy blue
& she said well now your Father's Day shopping is done,
that was cheap! I said, no, it's for my husband.
She said, right.

Does Father's Day make you sad? I ask him.
*Not now, but it did when I was a kid & a younger man.*
You mean back when you had that bad mustache?
*Yeah.* Maybe it wasn't Father's Day
that made you sad, I joke. Maybe it was the mustache.
I know what he means is *I never had a Dad.*
Then, *The man who taught me how to be a man died.*

I wasn't pregnant long enough to be taught how
to be a mother. I forget nipple ache like one
forgets the sound of a dead person's voice.

What do you forget? *I don't.*

Sometimes when it gets too cold overnight
& I cup my breast, palm against flesh,
it's almost like it was when I curled fetal, fetus
still there. I know what he means is *I only remember*
*it was the happiest we've ever been,*
*then the saddest.*

# Collecting Slights

Like beans in a can, *plink plink plink*
not unpleasant yet, but accumulating.

Sometimes you'll shake the can
like when the dog misbehaves,
paws on a visitor's chest,
water bowl tipped,
the wrong thing eaten,
a noise loud enough it scares you too.
Because you know that bean's a snub,
that's an unreturned call, that's
the end of something.

> You can imagine carefully lifting foil,
> making a bundle, revealing lightly-browned pastry
> ready for lemon curd or pudding—

Sometimes you'll pour the can
into a foil-lined pie pan, soft press
against fork-pricked dough.

Each prick a reminder
of what you're supposed to do:
stay down,
give no air, no puff up.

# The Poem About Infertility

I threw away potatoes, old & soft like
old & soft potatoes.

I smelled pickles on the bus, sour from someone's skin,
not from someone's lunch.

I'm glad I'm not the only one rotting.

———

There is one niece, there will be a nephew & twins.

Some ant species eat honeydew: sugary waste excreted
from sap-eating insects.

These ants make trades for honeydew meals.

Sisters-in-law, *here.* Take this.
Take whatever I have.
Make anything you need.

# Playground

I choose skins. I choose skin
every time, even cherry-scraped

knees, bloodied, & sweaty foreheads
of the concussed, thrown

from the witch's hat.
I will leap off the see-saw

when you're high in the air
just to see your bruises form.

I carry band-aids in my purse.
A measured length of wax paper, here—

use it on the slide. Go faster.
Break yourself. I'm broken too.

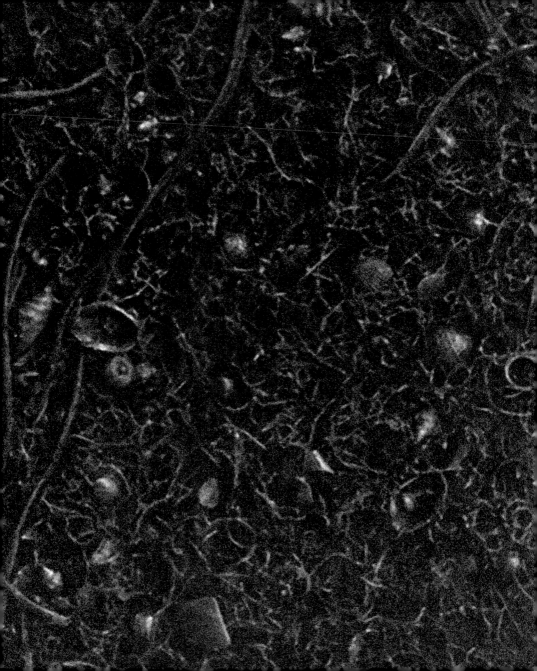

# The Feeder Said to Me

*It's home-cooked every time.*
He wants to make the thin woman
chubby, the chubby woman
fat, the fat woman supersized.

His rules are all about cleaning
your plate & keeping the spoon-
to-mouth rhythm as regular
as a man's self-controlled thrusts

at the beginning. I've heard
of others' rules: mandatory second
helpings, refusing requires punishment.
A slap to the face, not the ass.

Another says no utensils; he likes a sloppy
face. This feeder says to me, *Eat
as I say, not as I do,* as he exercises
around the kitchen, keeping a trim figure.

Squat-thrusts in front of the stove, isometric
bicep curls as he puts one grape
after another in his mouth, lips
like a kiss on the smooth red skin.

He gives a new twist to love bites:
I bite the food & he'll love me.
The feeder watches. He says, *Have you ever
been massaged between salad and main course?*

I turn my ample rump to him; he kneads
like bread dough & things are rising.
The feeder says he'll match my mastication.
With each clench of my teeth grinding,

he'll lick, get his tongue around what he wants.
The next course in front of me, steak tartare, egg
draped over raw meat. He says, *Circles contain more
possibilities than straight lines.*

The larger the egg,
the more enveloped the meat.

# Fat Girl at Weight Watchers Meeting

I'm supposed to tell
everyone I'm dieting
& give away pants
as they get too big.
They say if you feel bad
about your loss, go to
a grocery store, pick up a bag
of sugar, of flour, 10 lbs.—
that's what you used
to carry around your middle.
We clap for lost quarters
of pounds. This is the first time
I've lost more than sticks
of butter. When I slip,
when I cheat, I try
to imagine the alternatives.
But I fear the canula—
that lipo tool, long
like a princess's wand.
The doctor thrusts in & out

just under the skin
like fast sex & the sucking
in like a little girl's gasp
when she sees a prince.

# Fat Girl Confuses Food & Sex, Again

When I order a pizza, I am a sudden sexpot,
as if the pepperoni he's slicing
to top my pie is as powerful as a cock,
as if the sharp bite of good pepperoni rivals a thrust.
A power passes through the phone lines.
I am confident in my sexy voice, low & lusty—
he doesn't know I'll eat all sixteen slices, that I'll make love
to the hard crusty dough, let slick strings of cheese
dribble down my chin, pretending I was sexy
enough to make someone come.

# x = feathers, y = boards

english: light as a feather, stiff
as a board. she is a feather,

he is a board. logic proof: if light as a feather,
then stiff as a board.
what are the conditions of stiffness?

the boy will be stiff if & only stiff
if the girl is light as a feather & not bored.
chemistry & sex ed: if the girl is light as a feather,

as air, as feathery as air, then the boy will be
      stiff as a board

Pork is a verb, but only in slang dictionaries.

How many times have I used meat products as symbols?

*Their first date was at the mall at Christmastime.*

*He felt inferior as she eyed the summer sausage;*

*he knew nothing of her eating disorder.*

Pigs have thirty minute orgasms


& there are women who can suckle

their own tits—do they think about how

it's the advantage of flesh stretched enough?

I should try the male point-of-view:

*He wants oral auto-stimulation, can't get over*

*the fear of breaking his neck while curling down.*


I am the other white girl & I'm what's for dinner.

Sex on the kitchen table is for those exploring kink

for the first time. Think of the confusion of sperm

through pigs' penises, corkscrewed, like tails.

Entrees do dictate wine choice. I've never used white wine—

there's just something about the full body of red.

# I just did what I always do: eat.

I didn't want to go to the funeral home
because none of my clothes fit, because
my black pants are elastic-waisted.
I only feel happy wasted on cake.

She was still skinny like high school,
in a black blazer. I don't know
if it bothered me more that it took death
for me to see her again

or that her mother died from what
my mother survived. Tonight it was KFC,
mashed potatoes like a soothing balm.
Me & food, me & food, me

& food & a life of fuck-ups.
Though I never say *fuck-ups* because I can't
admit I'm not proud of this fat body.
I'm not crying for her mother

in a blue sweater in a box in December.
I'm crying for headaches I only heard about
over the phone, the surgery clip & run,
my mother's seizures, my mother's medicines.

An hour ago they said last goodbyes
for the night & it was probably home with aunts
& uncles, sandwiches from a deli tray, a moment
at the spot where she fell in the kitchen or laundry room.

It's what I imagine—the falling.
I'll find out later that she didn't fall, but collapsed
in the passenger seat of my friend's car. An aneurysm burst.
My mother—hers leaked for days. Repaired now, she seizes

every couple months, shakes & spits like she's trying
to purge the memory. If I were a different person,
I'd make myself vomit afterwards; instead I hold
every memory inside & grow bigger & bigger.

# Fat Girl on Winter Beach

Empty beach, out-of-season,
not a sunbather, not a bikini.
No one to touch the morning fog.
Tired of touching myself, but I never want
a man to touch me.
He might not like the cushion, or creativity
it takes to get legs over head.
Foamy caps circle at my feet like bath water
swirling to the drain & it's been five years
since I've been in water other than the tub.
The waves get rougher, harder
when approaching my thighs,
when I need to be in ecstasy, not thinking
of what is being seen: the bathing suit terror
of breasts not in place, cold nipples hard
but pointing down. Waves can't crash loud
enough, fast enough.
My weight is a darting mosquito buzzing
at my ear, impossible to ignore.
Soon the arrival of skinny swimmers, tanned muscles.
I want the sun. That hard candy ball.
I want it to melt me into the gritty sand.

# Not Quite Taste

December & we're sitting
in the Pleasure Bar in Bloomfield—
suddenly I feel bad about choosing a menu
that's moderately priced.
If I couldn't taste, or even smell, the food,
I'd spend as little as possible. What pleasure
would I find when only textures
bloom in my mouth, not flavors, not
subtleties of spice. She'll always refuse Jell-O
& spinach, slimy. Curry makes
her nose run. This evening it's
spaghetti, marinara preferable to meat—
imagine pushing a tomato chunk
to the roof of your mouth, the press
then release of more liquid. Ever since
her auto accident it's been like this. Now she smokes
& doesn't mind oral sex. There's vinaigrette
on her side salad—that something
that's not quite *taste* still catches her
at the jawline, near her ear—something
to remind her there was flavor in her other world.

I've asked her what she's able to savor,

she told me about soft-shell crabs,

how she waits for early May, velvet

crabs full of salt water, hard shells just shed.

Anticipation has been known to whet

many appetites. Dinners out really are

for the conversation. She'd never smell

the dust burning off a furnace the first cold night

in winter, never feel more or less

than the tomato on her tongue, smoothness

of raw skin, or fleshiness in the heat of sauce.

I can't wear the red
sweater anymore.

I've been getting emails
about cord blood.

I wonder if it's redder,
thicker, darker

than mother's blood,
is it *more*?

I lost weight from eating
healthy & learning

to control my sugars.
Wouldn't you want

when you're pregnant sweet,
sweet blood?

I will always confuse
succor & sucra-.

I read about the dangers
of artificial sweeteners then.

I read more into that red
sweater picture now.

It was Christmas.
No one knew.

I looked good at that party.
I didn't think I had that glow,

so early in the pregnancy.
I had too much

to think about, already
too much weight.

# Fair: Fun House Mirror

Fun house mirrors & fucking force us
to see every thing from every angle.

What did my face look like
when I was having one of those orgasms
he claimed I had, but didn't know I had?
I know what his face looked like when he grew tired.
I put my hand on top of his hand. He pulled back:
*yeah, yeah, do yourself.*

I stood in front of the mirror to see my lingerie.
I fell asleep waiting for him to come home.

I saw both our disappointments over the bed.
He untied my legs.

Really, Similac? I don't need
your Newborn Nutrition Kit
mailed from some warehouse
that keeps track of due dates
on a monster calendar plastered
on a cold concrete wall,
rows & rows of women's names
in each square, like grotesque Santa lists
of all the good girls, those who signed up
for mailings & apps to track fetal size,
always in fruited descriptions.
(*Your baby is a jackfruit!*)

      I was a bad girl.
I was a girl too old & a girl too fat.
I should give you away. I could
give you away to Kori or Sarah, both ready
to pop, to Tiffany, to Cristina, to Jaimie or Amy.
&, yeah, yeah, Similac, I know
it's not a wall calendar.

Your digital database is the "monster,"
pushing out twinned messages
to office & warehouse.

      It is your fault.
I'll cry myself to sleep two nights from now
expecting a jackfruit to pop out, on a spring,
umbilical, the music a soft *na-nah-na-na-nah*
in a little girl's whisper, *you can't catch me…*

# Fat Girl Has Regular Sex

We ate Jell-O poke cake in bed
one night after.  We brought it home
               from a church basement dinner,

plastic wrap over Cool Whip icing,
               whorls of orange inside.
*Definitions of regular: 1. belonging*

               *to a religious order*
He has made me say all those things
               I never thought I'd say: *oh god, oh oh*

*god.* I remember the *Sex*
               *and the City* movie scene, the girls
around the brunch table discussing frequency

               of sex. *2a. arranged*
*according to some established*
               *rule, principle, or type*

Charlotte, the Rules Girl, still put out
　　　　　two or three times a week.
Samantha will stop, drop & roll

　　　　　anytime, anywhere. We tried some X-
marks-the-spot position once, *2b. both*
　　　　　*equilateral and equiangular* both

on our sides, heads at opposing sides
　　　　　of the bed, our legs scissored
in & out of each other. It was in a book

　　　　　I bought before we did it,
*Big Big Love: A Sourcebook on Sex*
　　　　　*for People of Size and Those Who*

*Love Them,* when I thought it might
　　　　　take creativity to overcome two bellies
too big to smack against each other

　　　　　in any sexy way.
Miranda's marriage was ruined
　　　　　because she wanted their first romp

in six months to end quickly

      *3a. methodical <regular habits>*

& Steve admitted cheating.


      If that wasn't bad enough,

her friends chastised her for not

      trimming her pubes regularly


or enough. *3b. recurring at fixed intervals*

      *<a regular income>*

*<a regular churchgoer>*


      I know what's in his checkbook

& his prayer book. I know when he wants it.

      He knows I won't always


have shaved legs, pumiced heels.

      Carrie remained neutral

& wouldn't disclose how often Big gets big


      for her, although she said it's hot

when he does. She can be the every woman,

      her regular is every woman's regular,

unspoken, but understood.

      *4. normal, standard* I'd never seen
a written recipe for poke cake

      until recently on Pinterest.
It was passed from woman to woman,
         tips included along the way.

A fat McDonald's straw works best.
      Space the pokes at a regular interval
so the hot Jell-O bleeds

      into every corner of the cake.
*as absolute, complete*
      Advice for special positions

also only whispered in the past,
      wedding night instructions under veils
of white netting & feigned innocence.

      There are two kinds of people
in the world—those who buy books
      before milestones & those who read

sex help online. But no one flips through
　　　　　　a fat leather dictionary anymore
to find examples of use:


　　　　　　*Most days they follow a regular routine.*
*He is a regular contributor*
　　　　　　*to her boosted self-esteem.*


*We make regular use of each other.*
　　　　　　*The wallpaper in the bedroom*
*has a regular pattern of stripes.*

# Between My Legs & My Future

Unemployed & stealing watch
batteries for my vibrator,

I'm keeping time
between my legs & my future

husband is paying all the bills.
There's an extra layer

under my clothes. I'm fresh
from the fitting room.

Outside the store we're fogging
windows & he's peeling back

the years, through baby doll dresses,
through acid wash & neon.

Quincunx of pips on the fifth side
of a die: marriage is no prison               is no game

is an orchard, Euclidean lattice work: the middle dot
is me             center tree,
                     centered tree. You have my every back.

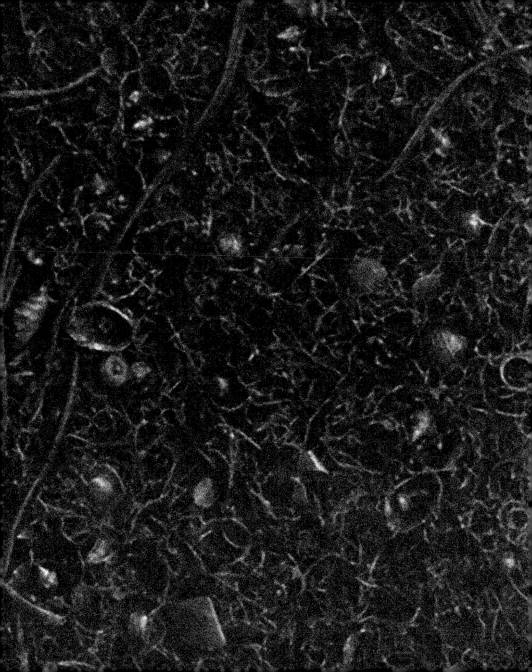

I want to argue,
*Enough is as good as a feast.*

But I can't even spit out
the first word, *enough,*
which would suffice.

He cuts me off before my mouth
can open, though open
is all he wants me to do.
& open wider still.

I see him grow
in anticipation of my body,
of food entering,
pushing past my lips,
with force if necessary.

He holds it in his palm.
It could be anything big,

anything to make me bigger.
Full: a slice of whatever I desire.

He holds it before me, an offering, a threat.

I push out the word *Now*.
Not knowing if I really want to say
*Now I'm leaving* or
*Now it's over.*

I repeat *Now*.

# What Hunger Was

I'm too bored to care
if cellophane wrappers crackle

during prayers, volunteer acolyte
in single seat hidden behind the lectern.

& then—candle douter between my legs,
eyes level with the cone,

thighs squeezing against the long handle—
snuffing out awakened ache.

I'm too rapt to care
if my breath quickens.

& then too hungry to forego
hunks of bread ripped from the loaf.

Signs at the tent screamed
YOU RING IT, YOU WIN IT...KNIVES!
I won four. I posed for pictures, blades open,
fanned across my cheek. The most dangerous
thing I'd ever done was break up with him.

Fool me once: I wouldn't know
his house by the Porsche he said was
in the driveway, there was never a Porsche
in the driveway. He didn't drive. No license.
It wasn't his house. It was his parents'
basement, musty, full of boxes, frequently flooded,
his bed tucked in a corner. Fool me twice:
*I can do better. I can do better.*
*I'm the best you can do.*

I agreed to a friendly gift exchange
for Christmas a month after.
Yellow gold charms & chains, a ring,
yellow gold, brash & cowardly,
jewelry I gave back because *no*,
I won't be that again.

# No One Has Touched Me So Hard
## It Calmed Me

I once woke a man at the end of the line.
I moved my fingers back & forth, just enough
to rustle his coat. He woke with such a start
I pressed my palm flat against his shoulder,
pushed him back into the bus seat.

I have to get leverage to rub my husband's back
as hard as he likes—prop myself on my elbow in bed.
His lower back is often in knots.
He moans like a porn star but believable
when I press my knuckles into his spine & move up

& up to his neck. The knots in my back
can only be untied with slow soft circles.
I bruise otherwise. He says I'm a wuss, he says
*I smack your ass harder than that when we're having sex.*
I say *I know.*

I fell inside Cogo's today. Pain on my right side, but it was the left side of my jeans coated in thick wax. The clerk, mop in hand, asked if it was still slippery. My nephew was baptized today. The pastor counted down perfumes, floral notes worth thousands per ounce. *Mary saved her whole life for the best perfume, saved so she could give Jesus the best, a pint of pure nard on his feet, some spilling on the floor.* The pastor implored us to not judge how others worship, to leave others with their choices, no matter how extravagant, to question only ourselves: *Why wait? Give the most now.* I walked from the store to the car in tears today. He was the most beautiful boy today. Instead of wiping his feet with our hair, we knelt on the floor with his toys around our knees, his every questioning cry met with our best answers. How did I fall today? Shoes untied? Then rolled onto my left side? Sometimes the best guess isn't even close. Nothing marking the freshly waxed floor? No. How many more days like today can I survive before I'm back on the floor, writhing, anything but still?

# Another Poem About Infertility

The body creates new,
until it doesn't.
Linings sloughed, shed,
bled. Snot, sand
in your eyes, fingernails,
toenails, flakes of skin
in the bed sheets.

The bed sheets are cool,
until they're not.
My back sweats against
the mattress, one leg
hanging over the side,
the other knee bent, foot
pressing down
so I can lift my hips to meet
your hand, fingers
hovering like kestrels
on the hunt.

The hunt continues
& orgasm swoops.
The contractions repeat,
replenish, until they don't.
The pleasure comes even if.
Even if the body
is the predator. Even if
I float up over the bed, hover
when you kneel between my legs
& begin.

Even the times I cry, it's fucking.
It's never been making love, all whispers
quiet like new fallen snow.
Even when it's slow—that's when
I'm guttural, *fuck* rising in my throat.

I would lie naked in a blizzard,
move with you, angelic & devilish,
if after we finished you warmed me,
tongue on my neck, tasting
what we've made: sweat, sweet.

I ate your balls
in Amarillo,
with jalapeño
garnish, fat,
whole, raw
peppers, green
like the foliage
we hadn't seen
since the Ozarks.
You ate my heart
in Chicago.
You said it tasted best
with everything
on the fork,
ramps, potato aioli,
even the strawberry,
red as excited flesh,
but soft,
waiting
for the first lick.

# The Infertile Couple

I touch my nose.

Last week I swapped an eggplant
I knew we'd let rot
      for three peppers in a plastic bag
      black-markered HOT.

I had just run my finger down the ribs,
      clearing the seeds.

                  it burns

It is the end of the first season
      with the CSA box (small share).

I put a blob of yogurt up my nose,

like a child,

you laugh & wipe it away.

We split the third pepper.

# What Not to Do

Don't text me pictures of your kids.
Don't ask me when we'll try again.
Don't tell me to use this as a springboard for weight loss.
Don't assume the days off work were a game.
I didn't want doctors three times the week after Christmas.

In the stall in the public restroom outside of the office,
I left clots & tissue.
You should have had the decency to say something, anything,
as the medics wheeled me to the elevators.

I left clots & tissue.
Sheet wrapped, spotted,
as the medics wheeled me to the elevators.

Sheet wrapped around my naked lower half, spotted.
I soaked pads in minutes. Lamaze-style through cramps.
As we were paying the co-pay at the ER check-out—
Don't ask if I had a good appointment.
Don't *this-might-be-for-the-best*.
Don't rephrase *this-might-be-for-the-best*.

I soaked pads in minutes.

Lamaze-style through cramps.

No D & C, but still that wasn't a good day.

Don't.

# Paper Birthday

Our baby is onion skin, not crisp
for folding into toy kites or airplanes,
but translucent, hard to see
in her white or canary colors, floating
just out of reach. She is thin,
bones also paper, scrolled
with only whispers inked
on the cotton fibers,
what her name would have been.

*August 6, 2014*

# Contemplating a Gift for a
# Pregnancy Announcement

I am the woman / mid-binge
I eat the children // those of complete
trimesters / children born
// not bled


                    you / then /          my best friend of the kitchen shears
my bridal registry // you /  now woman of the admission:

*I didn't always take weddings as seriously as I should have.*

you / then // hungry woman
        man walking out
        man // always walking out /

// woman / now loved / now announcing baby girl //

your daughter / burp cloths                    (if anything at all)
I might make her a precious child of white cotton onesies

// I take this very seriously / I am serious
        as scissors through my womb

# Coming to Terms with
# Gambling & Losing

Say you're a coin: to every
        problem you're two sides, the

yes & the won, the no & the
        two, you're up in the air & you

                see every mountain-top like blinking
        eyes, rolling view back to the
    road, the ocean, the
person on each rotation. You need

    lessons in the forget of forgive,
in the each of your eyes facing
        the flight of you're supposed to
    front, unflinching in the light of
        be over it.

# Notes for Whoever Will Take Care of Us When We're Old

I started wondering about you the Easter Sunday we put the dog down.

We have a second cousin the same age as the baby we lost.
What do you think it says about us that we never tried again?

I may ask him to get into bed slowly.
& though we ache, this won't be because of my joints or his back.

      (when we first lived together, every touch         every touch—)

He would lie down next to me, unfolding his body along the length of mine.

Slow.

It drove me wild.

# I'm Showing

I've had this belly for years, this belly now
speckled with insulin shot sites, some

in varying stages of bruise. I'm four weeks
& high glucose in the mornings. I'm five weeks

& internal ultrasound wand, the first condom
inside me in over a year. I'm six weeks

& craving spicy, hot sauce splashed
on every plate. I'm seven weeks

& you're the size of a blueberry, baby.
I'm high risk, at risk of callousing every fingertip

from up to seven tests a day. Fasting,
one hour after eating, bedtime.

We are careful to speak in ifs:
if all goes well at the next appointment,

if I'm able to carry to term.
But we've told everyone too

soon. I was on incompatible meds.
I stood at my mother's fridge before Sunday dinner

four weeks ago & ate pinched fingers full of blue cheese.
The journal I'm keeping isn't littered

with cravings of ice cream & pickles, isn't
interspersed with pictures of my belly with a placard

of the time frame held to the side.
When you start a pregnancy obese, your belly

isn't for show. What I'll share with you
is a log of glucose readings & carbs per meal.

I hope my fingertips heal. I want to save you,
but I'm afraid I'm carrying you like a bruise,

that you're soon to fade, but not before you turn
a sick yellow. Not before you leave me tender.

I have new bruises now:
on the back of my hand, blue
& small as forget-me-not petals
where the medic tried
to start a line en route
to the ER, after failing
at the inside of my elbow—
fluids needed since I was losing
so much blood.
The medic told me how his wife
miscarried twice before
they had their daughter.
He gently pushed my ring aside
so he could lay his hand flat
across the top of mine
as he tried to find the vein.
He failed again & I didn't get a line
until after the ER exam,
the plastic speculum clicking
into place, the collection
of blood into a white cup.

When I offered to take off
my ring, he joked that man
of mine better not find out
how easily I remove it.
I feel like I've let go
of too many things too easily.
I tried to keep you, baby.

She'd never thought of cradling
a blood clot in her palm,

or after pressing the darkest
center & finding it hard,
unyielding to her fingertip,

trying to see if it was the shape of anything

she'd seen time-lapsed on a doctor's wall.

———

I cradled blood.
I pressed the dark.

# Acknowledgments

Grateful acknowledgment is made to the editors of the following journals in which these poems, sometimes in earlier versions and/or with different titles, originally appeared:

*5AM* ("Writing the Fat Girl"); *Booth* ("Fat Girl Has Regular Sex"); *Bop Dead City* ("Another Poem About Infertility"); *The Chaffey Review* ("A Story of Girls"); *Chiron Review* ("Fat Girl Confuses Food & Sex, Again," "My Offal Honeymoon," and "What the Feeder Said to Me"); *Connotation Press: An Online Artifact* ("Post-Miscarriage: Day 55"); *Dressing Room Poetry Journal* ("On the Day My Husband is Assumed to be a Father by the Clerk in the Big & Tall Man's Clothing Store"); *elimae* ("The Poem About Infertility"); *The Emerson Review* ("The Rub"); *Gabby* ("Notes for Whoever Will Take Care of Us When We're Old"); *Harpur Palate* ("I Lost Our Baby"); *Hermeneutic Chaos* ("Before & After"); *Lilliput Review* ("Is No"); *The Lindenwood Review* ("Paper Birthday"); *Mead: The Magazine of Literature & Libations* ("I'm Showing"); *misfitmagazine.net* ("What Not to Do"); *Mobius: The Journal of Social Change* ("I just did what I always do: eat"); *Moon City Review* ("Fair: The Guesser"); *Nerve Cowboy* ("Fat Girl on Winter Beach" and "Post-Miscarriage: Day 74"); *The Paterson Literary Review* ("This Trouble of Curls"); *Pretty Owl Poetry* ("Between My Legs & My Future"); *Red Paint Hill Poetry Journal* ("Lost & Found Love Poem with Oranges & Trash"); *Revolution House* ("all day i dream about sex"); *scissors & spackle* ("Contemplating a

Gift for a Pregnancy Announcement"); *Stirring* ("Obedience Class"); *Stone Highway Review* ("Fat Girl at Weight Watchers Meeting" and "x = feathers, y = boards"); *Toad* ("Coming to Terms with Gambling & Losing"); *Uppagus* ("I'm Telling"); *U.S. 1 Worksheets* ("Fair: Ring Toss"); *Whiskey Island* ("Playground").

"all day i dream about sex" and "x = feathers, y = boards" are excerpted from the chapbook *When I Was a Girl* (Sundress Publications, 2014).

"Fat Girl on Baseball," "Fat Girl on Winter Beach," "Fat Girl Reads Her Horoscope," "Not Quite Taste," "What I Said to the Feeder," "What the Feeder Said to Me," and "Writing the Fat Girl" also appear in the chapbook *Nothing But Candy* (Liquid Paper Press, 2003).

"Fair: Fun House Mirror" was published in the Chapter and Verse feature of *Pittsburgh City Paper*, under the title "Fair (3)."

"Post-Miscarriage: Day 186" is included in *Voices from the Attic Volume XX* (The Carlow University Press, 2014).

Thank you, Jan Beatty, woman who is mad with encouragement and mad with support. Thank you, Lisa Alexander, A. M. Brant, Diane Kerr, Anne Rashid, and Joanne Samraney. Thank you to all of the Madwomen in the Attic. You are too many to name.

Thank you, Erin Elizabeth Smith and everyone at Sundress Publications. Thank you, Joseph Shields. Thank you, Michael Albright. Thank you, Michael Wurster and the Pittsburgh Poetry Exchange. Thank you, Kayla Sargeson. Thank you, James Allen Hall.

Thank you to my former teachers and former colleagues at the University of Pittsburgh and Indiana University. The older poems in this book owe a debt to your careful and insightful readings.

Thank you to everyone at YesYes Books, especially KMA Sullivan and Stevie Edwards, who saw something in these poems and pushed them and me to be better.

Thank you, Brenda Stumpf, for your beautiful work, for your textured and embodied and beautiful work.

Thank you, Matthew Nichelson, for patience while I posed.

Thank you to my family, especially my sister and best friend, Julia Jackson. I wrote this book just for the story.

Thank you, Mom, for everything. The greatest gift you and Dad gave me was showing me what marriage can be, what marriage should be.

Thank you, Mike. Simple is still best: I love you.

**Jennifer Jackson Berry** is the author of the full-length collection *The Feeder* (YesYes Books, 2016) and the chapbooks *When I Was a Girl* (Sundress Publications, 2014) and *Nothing But Candy* (Liquid Paper Press, 2003). She lives in Pittsburgh, Pennsylvania.

# Also from YesYes Books

FULL-LENGTH COLLECTIONS

*i be, but i ain't* by Aziza Barnes

*Love the Stranger* by Jay Deshpande

*Blues Triumphant* by Jonterri Gadson

*North of Order* by Nicholas Gulig

*Meet Me Here at Dawn* by Sophie Klahr

*I Don't Mind If You're Feeling Alone* by Thomas Patrick Levy

*If I Should Say I Have Hope* by Lynn Melnick

*some planet* by jamie mortara

*Boyishly* by Tanya Olson

*Pelican* by Emily O'Neill

*The Youngest Butcher in Illinois* by Robert Ostrom

*A New Language for Falling Out of Love* by Meghan Privitello

*American Barricade* by Danniel Schoonebeek

*The Anatomist* by Taryn Schwilling

*Panic Attack, USA* by Nate Slawson

*[insert] boy* by Danez Smith

*Man vs Sky* by Corey Zeller

*The Bones of Us* by J. Bradley
   [ *Art by Adam Scott Mazer* ]

*Frequencies: A Chapbook and Music Anthology, Volume 1*
  [ Speaking American *by Bob Hicok,*
  Lost July *by Molly Gaudry*
  *&* Burn *by Phillip B. Williams*
  *Plus downloadable music files from*
  *Sharon Van Etten, Here We Go Magic, and Outlands* ]


VINYL 45S
*A Print Chapbook Series*

*After* by Fatimah Asghar

*Dream with a Glass Chamber* by Aricka Foreman

*Pepper Girl* by Jonterri Gadson

*Bad Star* by Rebecca Hazelton

*Still, the Shore* by Keith Leonard

*Please Don't Leave Me Scarlett Johansson* by Thomas Patrick Levy

*Juned* by Jenn Marie Nunes

*A History of Flamboyance* by Justin Phillip Reed

*Inside My Electric City* by Caylin Capra-Thomas

*No* by Ocean Vuong


BLUE NOTE EDITION

*Beastgirl & Other Origin Myths* by Elizabeth Acevedo


COMPANION SERIES

*Inadequate Grave* by Brandon Courtney